must be
NiCE

your guide to growing
beyond the compare game

jason kotecki

JB!RD
ink

This book or any part thereof may not be reproduced or transmitted in any form or by any means without permission in writing from the publisher. For information, address JBiRD iNK, Ltd., PO Box 943, Sheboygan, WI 53082.

www.jbirdink.com

Scripture quotation taken from the Holy Bible, New International Version®, NIV® Copyright ©1973, 1978, 1984, 2011 by Biblica, Inc.® Used by permission. All rights reserved worldwide.

Cover and interior design and artwork by Jason Kotecki.

Library of Congress Control Number: 2023940726
Cataloging-in-Publication Data available upon request.

ISBN 978-0-9850732-6-8 (paperback)

ISBN 978-0-9850732-7-5 (e-book)

Books may be purchased for educational, business, or promotional use. For information on bulk purchases, please contact our team at 1-608-554-0803, or email store@escapeadulthood.com.

First Edition: August 2023

10 9 8 7 6 5 4 3 2 1

for St. Josephine Bakhita

a survivor with a grace-filled smile
who suffered unspeakable hell and
still found reasons to be grateful

contents

Introduction

The stage glowed with electricity and greatness.

Meanwhile, I sat there feeling dispirited and insignificant.

Even though I was surrounded by a thousand people, I felt very much alone, swallowed up in the dark belly of a cavernous ballroom.

The location was Philadelphia, at the annual convention for the National Speakers Association, of which I'd been a member for only a few years. The main stage was a showcase of the best of the best. It would have been inspiring had I not been swept up in an envy-fueled shame spiral.

After each speaker, I found myself muttering, "Must be nice."

Of course he's booked all the time; he played in the NBA and appeared on basketball cards. **Must be nice.**

She's got so many high-powered connections from working all those years as a Fortune 100 CEO. **Must be nice.**

I wish I could juggle and do backflips like that. **Must be nice.**

With each "must be nice," I became more cynical and more miserable. Left unchecked, this game can get grim, especially in the speaker world. Here is a terrible, horrible, no good, very bad example of what has probably crossed the mind of every professional speaker at some point:

Of course he's in demand; he's a blind, double-amputee cancer survivor who climbed Everest.

Twice.

Must. Be. Nice.

(Oof. Hello, Rock Bottom, nice to meet you.)

Suddenly, in the midst of my despair, I had a vision. There weren't angels or trumpets or locust-eating prophets, but it was a grace-filled moment of perspective and truth. Sitting there in the darkness, I was reminded of my artistic talent. It occurred to me that even though it's a gift few professional speakers possess, I was treating it as an afterthought, an unrelated skill that had nothing to do with saying words from a stage. I realized that were I to devote the time and attention to making my art an integral part of my unique selling proposition, someday I'd be on that main stage.

I sensed the inevitability of people in that future audience saying to themselves, "Of course he's a successful speaker. Being a great artist is a killer hook, and the ability to incorporate it into his storytelling and slides to drive home points, offer it to clients to help market their meetings, and sell it on merchandise that helps people remember the message for years to come is such an advantage!"

"Must be nice."

I had gotten good at noticing all the things I wasn't while missing the things I was. This revelation—to combine my art and speaking talents—might be obvious to you, as it was to the many speaker friends I shared it with, but it changed everything for me. Since that fateful convention, I've made art the cornerstone of our offerings, infusing it into everything I do. This is the spark that launched my career to a new level.

It's a natural human tendency to compare ourselves to others, especially people in our field. A psychologist named Leon Festinger came to this conclusion in 1954 with his social comparison theory. He stated that the more time someone spends on social media comparing their pathetic lives to their friends' highlight reels, the more likely that person is to eat an entire bag of Doritos.

Wait, no, that's not it.

What Leon *did* determine is that people compare and evaluate their opinions, accomplishments, and abilities by comparing themselves to others. That may seem obvious to us now, but it's interesting to go deeper into his findings. He noted that the more similar we are to another person, the more we tend to compare ourselves to them, like the way I did with other speakers.

Further, he suggested that the more important we view a group, the more pressure we feel to conform to that group's opinions and abilities. For me, it was a collection of people at the top of their game. If I can't measure up to them, what right do I have calling myself a professional?

Leon also pointed out that if we stop comparing ourselves to someone because it makes us feel bad, we deal with those feelings by mentally tearing that person down. We brand them as a hack, or maybe even a little evil, and rejoice when bad things befall them.

Pass over that bag of Doritos, will you?

> Do not spoil what you have by desiring what you have not; remember that what you now have was once among the things you only hoped for.
>
> —Epicurus

As you probably have deduced, the "must be nice" game is not exclusive to the speaking world. In your world, it might look like this:

She can eat whatever
she wants and never gains a pound.
Must be nice.

He gets straight As and he doesn't even have to study.
Must be nice.

She's pregnant again? I can't imagine it being that easy.
Must be nice.

They're always driving a new car because his company pays for it.
Must be nice.

She has all the time in the world to be involved in her kids' activities;
her husband has a great job and she doesn't have to work.
Must be nice.

Everything he touches turns to gold.
Must be nice.

Of course she is the top sales performer; she has a ton of contacts.
Must be nice.

Everybody likes him because he is a natural-born comedian.
He's the life of every party.
Must be nice.

She's tall and athletic and got a free ride to college because
she's a great volleyball player.
Must be nice.

He can afford a house like that because he's a carpenter
and can do all the labor himself.
Must be nice.

Of course they get to travel all the time; they have
two incomes and no kids.
Must be nice.

We identify someone we consider to be living a charmed life, and then we
tack on "must be nice" as our backhanded way of voicing our envy and
making excuses for ourselves.

It's also a
cop-out and
a tragic waste
of time.

Let's face it; as much as we may wish otherwise, life is not fair.

Call it what you want—luck, privilege, winning life's lottery, whatever—but the truth is this: inequality has existed for thousands of years, and it will exist in some form for thousands more. Creating a level playing field for everyone is a worthy pursuit we should all be striving for, but until we reach utopia, we must deal with the cards we've been dealt.

It's enticing to complain about being dealt a bad hand. It lets us off the hook. It's tempting to point fingers at institutions, blame the system, and cry foul over other people's unfair advantages. It's easy to play the victim.

And that might make you feel good, but it doesn't make you any better.

In her book *Tiny Beautiful Things*, Cheryl Strayed writes, "Nobody's going to do your life for you. You have to do it yourself, whether you're rich or poor, out of money or raking it in, the beneficiary of ridiculous fortune or terrible injustice. And you have to do it no matter what is true. No matter what is hard. No matter what unjust, sad, sucky things have befallen you. Self-pity is a dead-end road. You make the choice to drive down it. It's up to you to decide to stay parked there or to turn around and drive out."

You have to fight to be happy. It really is a choice, not something bestowed upon you by your fairy godmother or a genie in a lamp.

The first step is choosing to be accountable for your own life. I love this take from Gary Vaynerchuk, an entrepreneur and venture capitalist who said, "The mindset of accountability is what makes you win and makes you happy, whether it is true or not. The thought of taking on responsibility for everything that's not working is the win, whether you're right or wrong."

My friend Eliz survived a harrowing health emergency that left her with a compelling story. That story led to dozens of media appearances and launched her speaking career. So does that make the heart attack she had while pregnant with twins a "must be nice"?

I could write a million-page book with example after example of people from every walk of life, with every disadvantage you can name, who have overcome the odds to find happiness and experience joy. I'm sure you could add examples from your own life.

I'm not here to tell you it's easy, just that it's possible.

What these success stories all have in common is that the heroes didn't settle for playing the victim. They went to work making the most of what they had. And what they had was more than enough.

Jealousy and envy only distract us from a most important truth:

We all have a
"must be nice."

17

Everyone has unique gifts, circumstances, and experiences that they can leverage and benefit from. Some refer to it as an unfair advantage. In business, it could be a patent, a prime location, a charismatic founder, or an exclusive distribution deal with a big retailer. In everyday life, it might be your good looks, family connections to an influential person, or two decades of exhaustive experience in a particular field.

As I shared earlier, one of mine is my artistic ability. Your unfair advantage might be your grit, your intelligence, or your way with words. Maybe it's your position as an outsider who isn't held back by feeling the need to do things the way they've always been done. It could even be a heartbreaking past that enables you to empathize with people in similar situations in a way that no one else can.

We all have unfair advantages, but we rarely take time to identify them. And oftentimes, we overlook our greatest gifts because we undervalue the abilities that come easily to us. We fall into the trap of thinking if it's easy for us, it must be easy for everyone. (Hint: it's probably not.)

My goal is not to convince you that other people don't have advantages over you, but to lead you to uncover your own.

I was thinking about the American Revolutionary War the other day (because I like keeping up on current events), and a few things struck me.

I imagine it would have been easy for the American colonists to look at all the advantages held by the British and wallow in the land of Must Be Nice.

They have the most powerful navy in the whole world . . . must be nice.

They have way more professionally trained soldiers than we do . . . must be nice.

They have a ton of money to buy food, supplies, and mercenaries for hire . . . must be nice.

Their team has sweet red road uniforms . . . must be nice.

It's easy to lament other people's advantages and languish in jealousy and disappointment. But this only ensures defeat. Everyone has a must be nice (if not several), so we are better served spending our time figuring out what they are and using them to our full advantage.

That's exactly what those American revolutionaries did.

One must be nice of theirs was having home-field advantage. Their intimate knowledge of the nooks and crannies of the terrain benefited them. Also, many of the untrained soldiers were good marksmen, thanks to all their practice hunting small prey. And the biggest must be nice of all was that they were fighting for freedom and a better life for their families, while the British were merely doing their job.

In fact, this desire and passion helped give the Americans the will to identify rules that didn't exist and the courage to break them.

For instance, the British employed traditional firing line methods, which they were hesitant to abandon (hey, it worked for one hundred years!). The problem was it made them easy picking for snipers with long rifles who were hidden behind trees. And although the British held fast to the rule "thou shalt not shoot officers," the Americans determined this was one big fat #notarule and created confusion and weakness when they singled them out as the primary target.

I'd wager those fancy red coats made them easier to spot.

Consider these two lessons in your life, family, or organization.

First, just because something worked for a century (or a year) doesn't guarantee its success this year. The rules of yesterday can lead to ruin today.

Second, don't waste any time whining about someone else's must be nice.

Figure out yours and get to work.

Eight years after my private pity party in Philadelphia, I found myself backstage at Caesars Palace in Las Vegas. My wife Kim and I were preparing to open that very same speakers' convention with a main stage speech to our peers.

The title of the speech?

"Must Be Nice."

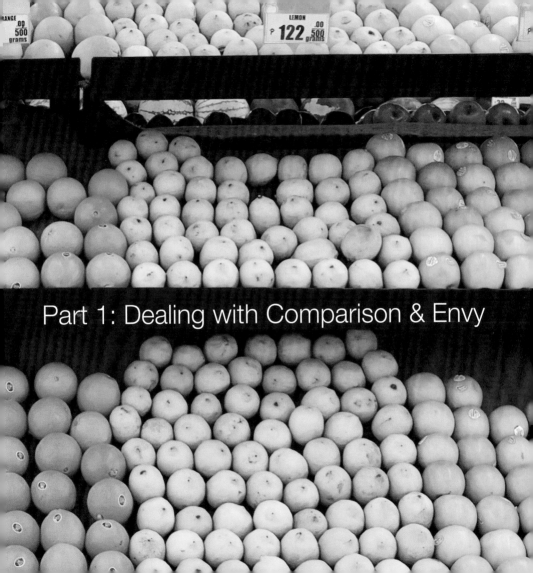

Part 1: Dealing with Comparison & Envy

The late, great Sean Stephenson once told me and Kim that "a life of compare leads to a life of despair." This wise observation was made even more powerful because Sean, who was born with osteogenesis imperfecta—aka brittle bone disease—stood three feet tall, had fragile bones, and used a wheelchair.

Unfortunately, comparison has established itself as one of our favorite pastimes. Our self-esteem plummets as we scroll through our social media feeds, absorbing everyone else's awesome life of perfection and adventure.

Folks often lament that social media is not authentic, that people only post the stuff that makes them look successful and happy.

Well, duh.

I'm reminded of Christmas letters, the endangered once-a-year tradition people use to share the accomplishments and happy milestones enjoyed over the past year. For generations, the Christmas letter served as a record of our greatest hits.

Now, social media is the new Christmas letter, written in real time over the entire year. I think that's a wonderful way to use social media, even if it doesn't tell the whole story. (Seriously, no one wants to read the play-by-play status updates of your messy divorce or to see photos of your nasty bruise.)

We don't need to change what we post; we just need to change our perception of what's being posted. The solution is a simple shift in perspective.

We need to stop comparing our everyday life to other people's greatest hits

Because the danger—and miserable onset of Adultitis—comes when we start assuming everyone else has it together. This mindset can lead to envy, jealousy, and depression, all of which are uglier than that indigo Argentina-shaped bruise of yours.

It's been said that comparison is the thief of joy.

The sneaky thing is, we can compare our burdens just as easily as we compare our blessings, making it an equal opportunity trap. We need to be reminded that when all we see is the highlight reel, we miss the shortcomings that drive people crazy and the hard battles they are quietly fighting. Like my dad says, "The grass may look greener on the other side, but it still has to be cut."

[Full disclosure: The adorable photo here was taken after a dinner out that also included a spilled drink, some sibling rivalry, and lots of whining. None of which are pictured.]

On our hardest days, in the face of overwhelming adversity, it's tempting to think we've been given a raw deal. We'd gladly trade our pile of problems with someone else's for a day. When I feel that way, I recall a popular old parable—author unknown—called "Is Your Cross Too Heavy to Bear?":

> The young man was at the end of his rope. Seeing no way out, he dropped to his knees in prayer. "Lord, I can't go on," he said. "I have too heavy a cross to bear." The Lord replied, "My son, if you can't bear its weight, just place your cross inside this room. Then, open that other door and pick out any cross you wish." The man was filled with relief and said, "Thank you, Lord," and he did as he was told.
>
> Upon entering the other room, he saw many crosses; some so large the tops were not visible. Then, he spotted a tiny cross leaning against a far wall. "I'd like that one, Lord," he whispered. The Lord replied, "My son, that is the cross you just brought in."

When I am frustrated by my predicament, it helps me to think about Sean, or my father-in-law, Gary, who struggled with the painful and crippling effects of severe rheumatoid arthritis for most of his adult life. Suddenly, my problems feel more manageable and I feel more fortunate.

Regardless of its form, comparison is too often a distraction holding us back. Camille DeAngelis, author of *Life Without Envy*, warns, "If you keep wanting what someone else has, you can't grow into everything you could be."

Indeed, you have a unique mission no one else can complete. Comparison is our enemy when it distracts us from our mission and leaves us feeling intimidated, afraid, and unworthy.

I feel that way sometimes, especially when I'm about to speak to an audience outside my comfort zone. I have to remind myself that yes, the people in the seats may have experience, social status, intelligence, or degrees that exceed my own, but I have something valuable to contribute, too. My unique perspective may be just what someone needs to hear that day.

Too often, we judge our weaknesses against other people's strengths. Not only does this make us feel insignificant; it also undermines our ability to serve in a way only we can.

I recall an opportunity I had to speak at a national conference in Tampa. The keynote speaker the day before my presentation was a household name. He was way more famous with a way more impressive resumé. I almost talked myself into leaving the event. Why do I have to follow him? What could I offer this crowd? I convinced myself I'd be a major letdown.

Thankfully, I dug deep into my well of faith and gave myself a pep talk. I reminded myself that I was there for a reason, and my job was not to match the previous speaker, only to be the best me I was capable of being.

And the speech went great. I even had a handful of people tell me how disappointed they were with the previous day's speaker, that he was rude and arrogant. The president of the organization that sponsored my talk told me he was never prouder to be the sponsor of a presenter.

Good thing I didn't leave after all.

I once had the privilege of being in the audience for a speech by Brené Brown at the World Domination Summit in Portland. As she vulnerably shared her own uneasiness with being on that stage, she offered an insight that served as a reminder to her and to each of us: "No one belongs here more than me."

I like that.

Confidence is not feeling like you're better than everyone else.

That's cockiness.

Confidence is the deep-seated belief that no one is better than you.

Which leads me to the color **brown.**

In the pantheon of crayon colors, **brown** rarely gets much love.

Red and blue seem to have the best publicists, for they are the colors most widely named as people's favorites. But brown is handy for drawing trees, hair, skin, and many animals. (And let's not forget chocolate!) Although we may have our favorites, no color is better or more useful than the others. Each is unique and equally great.

Although we all have different backgrounds, viewpoints, and strengths and talents, we each have a distinct brand of magic we are called to unleash on the world.

We need you to do your part. We need your magic.

Because if you remove one crayon from the box, our world becomes a little less beautiful.

Comparison can definitely be a joy stealer. But it can also come in handy.

The instinct to look to other people for information about ourselves is hardwired into us. One of the things that sets humans apart as a species is our capacity for self-reflection and the fundamental need to understand ourselves. But the only way to evaluate ourselves is in relation to something else.

You know—through comparison.

Sometimes we need it to understand how good we actually are. So comparison is positive when used as a benchmark for growth, like when you look at your past self versus your current self versus your future self. Or maybe you look up to someone as a source of motivation to get to the next level.

But when comparison shifts into envy or jealousy . . . Houston, we have problem.

It's the difference between self-improvement and self-esteem.

Using comparison to discover where to improve: good!

Using comparison to make yourself feel better about yourself: not so much!

So what do we do about this conundrum?

Remember back in school, when your class was taking a test and the teacher would exhort, "Eyes on your own work!"

As I was an amazing student (and because my parents may be reading this), I knew this warning was never aimed at me. But you know what? I wish I had someone like this in my life now, periodically reminding me to keep my eyes on my own work.

You see, my ability to keep my eyes on my own work relates directly to my level of happiness. I could use someone to slap my knuckles with a ruler anytime I got jealous over an opportunity given to someone else that I felt I deserved. When my eyes linger too long on the fruits of someone else's success, I can easily feel discontented, frustrated, aimless, impatient, and disappointed in myself—ultimately like a failure.

Scrolling through Instagram or your Facebook feed is just one focused session of peeping into everyone else's work. It can be toxic.

W. L. Sheldon, a well-known lecturer in the nineteenth century said, "There is nothing noble in being superior to some other man. The true nobility is in being superior to your previous self."

Brilliant! When I am focused on the game I'm playing, working on achieving my goals that firmly align with my why, and competing against my past self, things are rocking and rolling. I'm happy, content, and invigorated with purpose, excited to tackle the challenges ahead.

I'm more fulfilled when I'm breaking my own records, not the ones my neighbor has set. And I'm happier when I'm focusing on what brings me joy, not what floats my neighbor's boat.

Turns out a big key to happiness and the best way to remain unaffected by someone else's bigger house, better wardrobe, nicer car, higher-paying job, more successful kids, fancier vacation, more prestigious client, or larger bank account is simple.

Keep your eyes on your own work.

Here are a few other ways to help curb the negative effects of comparison:

Curate a healthy social media feed. A few years ago, I decided that my Instagram feed would only be filled with art and artists that inspire me. I culled my feed from everything that didn't meet those criteria. That small choice made my life a lot better. You get to decide who is allowed into your social media feed. You don't have to follow everyone who follows you, and you can drop people who are always bragging, who trigger that tinge of envy within you, or who post photos of their bruises.

Celebrate your achievements. When I achieve a milestone, I am more inclined to keep my head down and keep pushing toward the next goal than throw a party for myself. But over the years, I have learned how important it is to the long game to slow down and "treat yo self" from time to time. Celebrating your wins is an important and healthy part of the journey.

Count your blessings. I don't know about you, but I could use a daily reminder to count my blessings, not how many my neighbor has. We'll talk more about the surprising power of gratitude later, but it's hard to feel bad when you're thinking about all the good stuff going on in your life. Our minds can hold only one thought at a time. When you concentrate on your blessings, there's no room for comparison.

Have a social media detox. You are not required to start each day checking in on everyone who climbed Mount Everest while you hit the snooze bar three times. There is no law requiring you to end your day staring into the blue light of your phone as you fall asleep. On the other hand, you don't have to delete all your accounts and throw your phone into Mount Doom in Mordor. You can simply take a break for a week or two and enjoy the return of balance it brings to your life.

Kay Wills Wyma, author of *I'm Happy for You,* offers this handy CTRL-ALT-DEL method for dealing with comparison:

CTRL: Control the thought process by pausing to recognize the problem.

ALT: Consider an alternative perspective.

DEL: Eliminate comparison—or at least tone it down.

Kay says, "Looking at what we lack prevents us from noticing how sweet the world already is. But when we shift our focus from what could be to what actually is, we find extraordinary joy in our ordinary lives."

Clearly, our relationship with comparison is complicated. Perhaps the worst side effect is when it causes us to give up before we even begin. Or when we tell ourselves we'll never be as good as someone else or achieve what they've been able to accomplish.

I consider myself a professional reminderer. My high school guidance counselor never mentioned it to me as a job option, but I have somehow made a living reminding people of stuff they already know.

So allow me to take this moment to remind you that **most things fail.**

Most books aren't bestsellers. Most businesses don't make it more than a few years. Most podcasts don't see five episodes. Most New Year's resolutions disappear faster than a sleeve of Thin Mint Girl Scout cookies.

Success stories are noteworthy, which is why we see them trumpeted in the news and on social media. The news doesn't report the 763 million ideas that were tried and didn't work out yesterday. No reporter is live on location to tell us, "Margaret Schlub started her new diet this morning with a slice of avocado toast. She is currently polishing off an entire stuffed crust pizza by herself."

We know this. But we somehow forget all this when we see someone succeed, responding with the obligatory "must be nice."

Envy is the monster lurking behind the sarcasm of our must be nice laments.

Let me tell you why envy is the worst.

Traditionally regarded as one of the seven deadly sins, envy is unique in that it offers no pleasure. Philosopher Jeff Cook argues that whereas lust, greed, anger, sloth, gluttony, and pride all offer the sinner the pleasures of sex, money, power, ease, food, or self-esteem, envy offers the sinner nothing but misery.

In the journal *Dappled Things,* Mark Watney reflects on the famous parable of the prodigal son. The parable focuses on the younger of two sons who wastes his inheritance on booze and floozies, only to return home a humbled man welcomed by his father with open arms. Watney observes:

Yet this older son—who only appears at the end of the parable—is filled with resentment and misery because his father welcomed back his wasteful younger son by slaughtering the delicious "fatted calf." But note this: he is not miserable because he didn't get a fatted calf; he is miserable because his younger brother did. And not even a thousand fatted calves would make him happy now. He does not want just a fatted calf—he wants his younger brother to not have a fatted calf.

raSPberRies to ya

Fortunately, with a little reframing that feels a lot like jujitsu, it's possible to turn envy into a useful tool. Think of it like a bull in a China shop. Or to be more original, a toddler in a Fabergé egg factory. It's clumsy, rude, and violent. But it can be tamed. You can do that by asking yourself some questions anytime envy enters your egg factory.

First, think of someone who has recently triggered envy within you. Maybe it's a friend, a coworker, or a famous person living the life of your dreams. **What do they have that makes you wish you could trade places with them? Write down the first thing that comes to mind:**

There's a good chance you both have a thing or two in common, which is why it feels possible for you to have what they have. After all, where there is no feeling of possibility, there is no envy. For example, I might find it interesting to experience pregnancy and childbirth, but since it's not possible for me, envy never pops up when I see a pregnant lady as it might for a woman who has struggled to conceive. **So, what do you and this person you've identified have in common?**

Now, a little honest introspection will reveal that you also have many differences, including skills, aptitudes, interests, and desires. This person might have advantages that are out of your control (several inches taller, math wunderkind, twenty years older, twenty years younger, etc.) or that you don't want to emulate (willing to work eighteen hours a day, has no social life, lives in a rural area/big city/different country, etc.).

Write down some ways you are not equal. What qualities do they have that you lack? It's possible that at this stage, you may decide it's more appropriate to admire them or pity them rather than envy them.

As we discussed earlier, we often look at other people's greatest hits, and then stop looking. But as awesome as another person's life may appear, there are always downsides, difficulties, and challenges we don't see at first glance. For instance, I might envy the glut of Super Bowl rings Tom Brady collected in his career of superhuman length, but I also am not fired up about a strict diet that considers one slice of pizza after a Super Bowl victory a treat.

To those who don't know our story, it would be easy for someone to say it must be nice that Kim and I live in our dream home on Lake Michigan. And they'd be right! But it also took us twenty years, tons of work, and lots of sacrifices.

envy sees the sea but not the rocks.
—Russian proverb

Write down any rocks this person you envy might have to deal with in their life. **Can you think of any examples why it would be weird, impossible, or even undesirable to be that person?**

Too Hot.   Too Cold.   Just Right.

50

Now let's put the shoe on the other foot. Believe it or not, they might wish they had some of your must be nices. I bet a lot of celebrities wish they didn't have to see a magazine in a checkout line with a photo of themselves looking like a zombie that just got off a roller coaster. **Is there something—even one thing— you could imagine them envying about your life?**

Now let's be real. As uncomfortable as it may be to admit, it's also possible that the reason this person has what you want is because they've worked harder than you, sacrificed more than you, or have been doing it longer than you have.

If so, you have two options.

First, if the answer is yes to any of these questions, you have the option of using this opportunity as motivation to double down: Are you willing to put in the hours? Invest your life savings? Abstain from the calories? Accumulate the sweat?

And if the answer is no, then option two is simple:

stop wanting what other people have if you're not willing to do what they've done.

Too harsh? The truth may hurt, but it can also set us free.

There is a third option—to keep feeling envious—but that just permits poison to ferment and fester in your life. Let's not do that, okay?

Hopefully this activity is helping you see the clumsy impulsiveness of envy revealing itself. It is such an overpowering force that when we feel it toward someone, we usually covet their entire life, when in fact there is only a small aspect we desire, and we miss some crucial context.

do the work

The most important reason for taming envy is that when our attention is focused on someone else's charmed life, we squander the chance to create our own and make the world better.

By examining our envy under a microscope, we can diffuse its rage and turn it into a tool to help us succeed.

Author Danielle LaPorte wrote, "Who or what inspires you? You are what you're attracted to. Whatever is appealing to you lives within you." I'd add that like inspiration, envy sends a useful signal—albeit a crude one—about what you want and how to get there.

What is a quality about this person that you admire and could learn from?

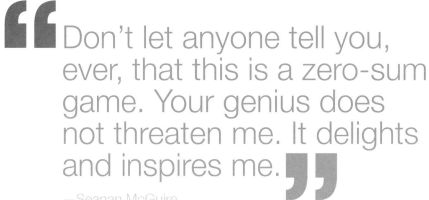

> "Don't let anyone tell you, ever, that this is a zero-sum game. Your genius does not threaten me. It delights and inspires me."
> —Seanan McGuire

Now ask yourself, **"What would I need to do to adopt that quality in my life?"**

Now we're getting somewhere useful.
Thanks, envy.

It's also useful to think of all the times in your life you've yearned for something that you eventually got, but it didn't improve your life as much as you'd anticipated.

I love this observation my friend Stephen Shapiro makes in his book *Goal-Free Living:*

> *We live in a society where we have convinced ourselves we need more. Life won't be complete until I have that plasma screen. I will be happy when I get a new car. I will be happy when I can afford a larger house. It's only been in recent times that many of these things even existed.*
>
> *The car was not popular until the early 1900s when Henry Ford produced the Model T. Television did not become popular until the 1950s. The computer, the Internet, broadband, and cell phones are all very new phenomena. Were people unhappy before these items were available? Of course not. Are we happier now that we have all of these inventions? Doubtful.*

Envy can be a useful signpost, but it rarely predicts what will make us happy in the long run.

Being able to learn what envy can teach us is a healthy place to be. But there is an even better, Jedi Master level available, and it is this: turning into the number one cheerleader of the person we once envied.

"Cheering for others is always the right thing, period. Their winning isn't coming out of yours."

—Gary Vaynerchuk

Taking the spotlight off yourself by thinking about how you can cheer people on, be a blessing to them, and help them get where they want to go turns the tables on envy. It ultimately helps both parties.

Bertrand Russell agrees: "Whoever wishes to increase human happiness must wish to increase admiration."

I like how Kay Wills Wyma describes it in her book *I'm Happy for You:*

> *If you can for a moment get your eyes off yourself and actually celebrate someone else's work, achievement, talent—anything, even something as small as complementing their shoes—it might make the person feel good, but it actually helps you. . . . Being preoccupied with how we measure up personally leads to either pride or humiliation, whereas choosing to focus on and congratulate the other person lifts us both up. . . . The hardest part is that we have to mean it. . . . [In the shift of] moving our eyes off self to consider others . . . in saying, or at least thinking, I'm happy for you—we move from comparison to compassion.*

You might not feel like aiding a perceived adversary. It might feel counterintuitive rooting for someone to win a prize you want to receive. Fortunately, feelings don't get the final say. When we choose to celebrate the success of others, we win in the end.

As writer Hannah Brencher confirms in her book *Fighting Forward,* "Stepping into someone else's race to push them forward is one of the more fulfilling tasks you will ever take part in."

Whether or not you can get yourself to cheer on someone you envy, it's imperative that you at least stop beating yourself up. I made a painting to help myself do that by reminding me about a few things...

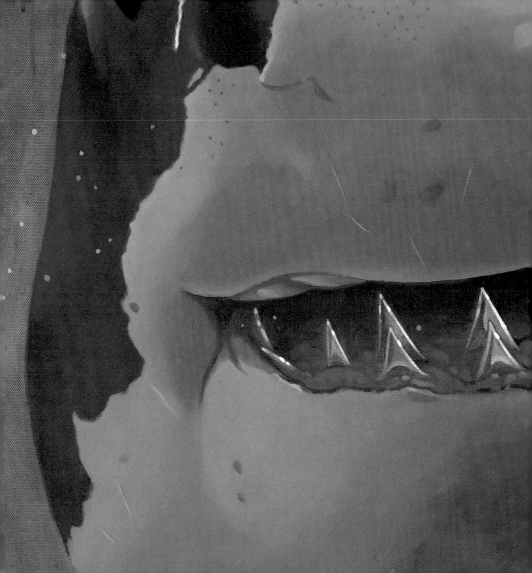

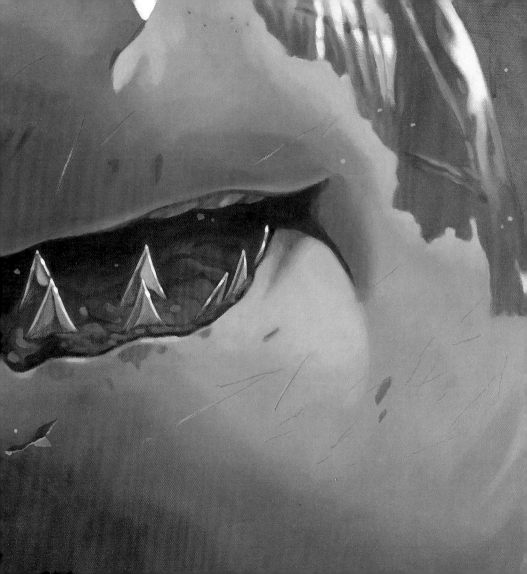

First, this shark is awesome. Just look at his gold teeth. Obviously, the male sharks want to be him and all the ladies want to be with him. That he is a success is a foregone conclusion.

The joke is on the shark, though, because these teeth are not long for this world. You see, sharks continually shed their teeth—with some shedding approximately thirty-five thousand teeth in a lifetime! That's a lot of lost bling. What a shame!

The tragedy, though, is that gold grill or no, he already was great. He just didn't believe it.

I don't know about you, but I make this mistake all the time.

I chase after shiny objects that don't last to prove my worth, even though deep down I don't always feel so worthy.

When I was in seventh grade, I would have given anything for a pair of Air Jordans. I didn't feel cool but was certain these shoes would make up for it. Maybe they'd distract the girls from my pimples, awkwardness, and bus windshield–sized glasses. Alas, I never got them. It's just as well because I now question their effectiveness, and they wouldn't have fit me a year later anyway.

Back at the turn of the century, Apple came out with the iBook. The lime green one was, in the immortal words of '80s icon Ferris Bueller, "So choice." I printed a picture of one and put it on my vision board, imagining that possessing it would make me hip. Never got it. Of course, if I still had it today, it would be little more than a decorative doorstep.

I have dreams of owning a Porsche 911 convertible someday. I think it is a beautiful car, and I love driving convertibles (my dad used to have one). But sometimes I wonder if the real reason I want it is to show everyone how great and successful I am.

My faith teaches me that I am wonderfully made in the image of my Creator. That's flattering but frankly hard to believe most days. After all, I wear bifocals now. My hair is thinning. I eat lots and lots of gluten.

Interestingly, my perspective changes when I think about my kids. Are they perfect? Hells no. (They take after their old man, after all.) But they are great. It's not hard for me to see their amazing qualities. And the kind of shoes they're wearing has nothing to do with it.

Why is it so easy to see the positive traits of others and so hard to see them in ourselves?

Sure, there are people out there who are too big for their britches. But even in those cases, once you collect a certain amount of wisdom, you realize that the bombast and overconfidence are merely masking their own unworthiness.

Indeed, most of us are overwhelmed by our flaws and sell ourselves short. We believe the TV and magazine ads that tell us we need to fix this, tuck that, and acquire the new gizmo to feel complete. I don't know if you can relate, but I often feel suffocated by thoughts that I'm not enough.

Not **smart** enough.

Not **talented** enough.

Not **brave** enough.

Each of those "not enoughs" is like a weed, crowding out the truth:

You belong here.

you don't have to act cool. you already ARE.

kotecki

A few years after that shame-spiral-turned-revelatory convention in Philadelphia, I attended a workshop with twenty-four fellow speakers, hosted by a couple of speaking industry titans. We met to improve our storytelling skills. As part of the agenda, everyone was required to do five minutes of material in front of the group, after which we received advice to help us improve.

I was intimidated by the level of talent in the room. I wondered if I belonged. I was nervous. But it didn't take long for me to realize something profound:

Everybody else was nervous, too.

Keep in mind these were some of the best speakers in the world. Folks you've seen on TV, some who have been elected to the Speaker Hall of Fame and have wowed audiences in the most prestigious venues.

And everybody was at least a little nervous. A small piece of each of us wondered if we belonged in that room.

It gave me a great sense of calm knowing I wasn't the only one. I was also perplexed, wondering what some of my heroes could be nervous about. But then I began to wonder, what did I have to be nervous about?

How much time and energy do we waste doubting ourselves, wondering if we deserve to be in the room?

Thomas Edison has been attributed with saying,

> "If we did all the things we are capable of, we would literally **astound** ourselves."

This is true. The potential within each one of us is enormous. But I'll go one step further. I say that we'd be astounded if we knew how good we already are.

Maybe the marketing messages we've been bombarded with over the years have convinced us that we really aren't good enough. Maybe we haven't received enough positive compliments. Maybe we think the people who compliment us are just being nice, or don't know the real us.

If you're still reading this...

STOP

Stop thinking you're not good enough.

You belong in the room.

You matter.

We desperately need you to believe this, because we need your contribution.

You have a special brand of awesome that no one else has.

Believing it doesn't exist dishonors the gifts you have to share.

You may not be as good as you could be, but you are already way better than you think you are.

You and me, we are already great. And not in some lame, everybody-gets-a-participation-trophy way.

Seriously, do you know the odds of you even being here? After hearing a TEDx talk by author Mel Robbins in which she mentioned the probability of being born, Dr. Ali Binazir was inspired to crunch the numbers. When you factor in the probability of your dad meeting your mom . . .

> . . . and that they stayed together long enough to have a kid . . .

> . . . and that one of the one hundred thousand eggs your mom produces in her lifetime . . .

> . . . met one of the four trillion sperm your dad made during the years you could have been born . . .

> . . . there is a 1 in 400,000,000,000,000,000 (1 in 400 quadrillion) chance of you being alive.

By the way, the chance of you being killed by a shark are about 1 in 4,000,000.[1]

Source: The International Shark Attack File (ISAF)
https://www.floridamuseum.ufl.edu/shark-attacks/odds/compare-risk/death

,000,000,000

You overcame **1** in **400** quadrillion odds to be born.

Must be nice.

Statistically, you are a miracle. Having beaten odds like that suggests there is a reason you are here. And indeed, there is. You have something to offer that the world needs.

You see, the real reason for your greatness is that you were purposefully and wonderfully made by a loving God. Within you—amidst any so-called flaws you dwell on—is a spark of something divine. That, my friend, makes you priceless.

The good thing about this feeling of "not enough" is that it helps us make room for God. His power is made perfect in our weakness. He picks up the slack and nullifies our deficiencies. We are truly in danger when we think we can do this thing called life alone.

> "When I was a child my parents loved me not because I was good but because I was Madeleine, their child. I loved them, and I wanted to please them, but their love of me did not have to be earned. Neither does the love of God. We are loved because we are his children, because we are."
> —Madeleine L'Engle

Learn the lesson this shark didn't. You don't have to keep trying to prove yourself. You can just be.

You may not be perfect, but you are already great.

Gold teeth or no.

And that's amazing news, because the secret to success and happiness is not by comparing yourself to others, or by trying to be something you're not, but by embracing your exceptional brand of originality.

Have you ever noticed you can always tell whether a child's drawing was actually drawn by a child or an adult?

Advertisements, signage, or product packaging will sometimes convey a childlike quality by including elements supposedly drawn by a kid. Most times, the drawing is done by a grown-up mimicking a child's drawing. And you can tell it's a fake.

Why is that?

It's because the grown-up is trying to be something he or she is not. A real child's drawing contains the bold, uninhibited, and unconventional expressiveness of that child. An adult can try to copy that spirit, but it is a fool's game. The adult is burdened with too many preconceived notions: what color something is supposed to be, what shape something is, how big it should be in relation to the other objects. Even though a grown-up may try to ignore those learned observations— by making the sun a yellow scribble or the house a wobbly square—she might not even consider making the trees float, which may be an obvious choice for a child.

Usually, the grown-up ends up with an image that looks kind of like something a child would draw, but it's always just a bit off, making it glaringly inauthentic.

"To be nobody-but-yourself—in a world which is doing its best, night and day, to make you everybody else—means to fight the hardest battle which any human being can fight; and never stop fighting."

—E.E. Cummings

Nothing beats an original.

This is a drawing of a character created by my daughter, Virginia Rose. His name is Big. He lives in the clouds and comes down to give people hugs.

We run into the same problem when we imitate someone else instead of being ourselves. When we try to fit into a career that doesn't suit us, mirror the journey of a personal hero, or follow in our father's footsteps, no matter how well we do it, something will always be just a bit off. People can tell, and more importantly, we can feel it. Ironically, the reason we can't pull off successfully mimicking someone else is because too much of "us" gets in the way.

The trick isn't doing what everyone else is doing. The trick is being more you. Or as my friend Amy says, "I try to be abundantly me."

Like a child with a blackboard and a fat piece of chalk, we need to open the floodgates and let the "us" run free.

Once, when Kim and I were dancing at a party at the end of a business conference, a colleague noted our silly moves and Kim's bare feet and exclaimed, "This is so on brand for you!" One might have taken her statement to mean that we were manufacturing something, but it was just us being us.

It is only when we boldly go in our own direction, tap into our mix of unique talents, and embrace our wonderful idiosyncrasies that we can fashion a life that is an authentic and inspiring work of art. It's always better to be a first-rate you than a second-rate somebody else.

Or as my friend Scott observes...

"Cover bands never make it into the Rock & Roll Hall of Fame."

—Scott Ginsberg

There is power in your

That's what we want to see.

And it's exactly what the world needs.

" Imitation is
the sincerest form
of boring. **"**

—Jason Kotecki

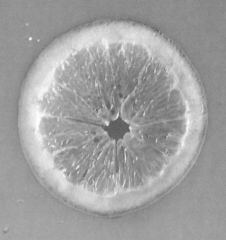

Part 2: How to Find Your Must Be Nice

Have you ever had one of those days when you're angry at everything and nothing in particular? I had one recently and went for a walk to melt my anxiety. Two laps around a spacious field of wildflowers near my home released some endorphins, but it didn't make a dent in my foul mood.

I pulled out my earbuds and fired up a playlist on my phone populated with praise music. My soul began to lift.

Then I came upon an older man driving a golf cart along the path, with a woman of a similar age as his passenger. She appeared to have some cognitive challenges as she seemed pretty unresponsive. I guessed they were husband and wife. Perhaps he had been visiting her in the nearby mental health center and decided to take her for a ride on what was a beautiful day.

They were together, but not really. At least not in the way my wife and I are when we go for a ride together, talking all the

way. In that couple, silently traversing fields of wildflowers under the late-summer sun, I saw not only true love, deep loyalty, and the kind of frail but breathtaking beauty that arises only from brokenness; I also saw a million reasons to be thankful. My eyes were opened to a treasury of blessings I'd been blind to an hour before. I turned off the path and headed back home, returning a happier, more hopeful person than the one who left.

Anxiety is the dominant emotion of our time. It's a constant companion as we slog through our days, scan the headlines, and scroll through our social media feeds.

Fortunately, there is a cure and it doesn't cost a dime.

The antidote to anxiety is **gratitude**.

"When eating fruit, remember the one who planted the tree."

—Vietnamese Proverb

If you are feeling anxious, make a list of ten things you are grateful for. It's impossible to do this and not feel better. I **double-dog dare you** to make a list of one hundred and tell me your mood is not transformed.

Anxiety is anticipating the bad in what may never happen.

Gratitude is acknowledging the good in what already has happened.

> **If the only prayer you said was thank you, that would be enough.**
>
> —Meister Eckhart

Why does gratitude make us feel better? This painting explores this phenomenon while addressing another. The photo I used as reference was taken during my family's whale-watching tour in Mexico. I'm still amazed that we saw a humpback whale breach. I'm also amazed that mankind still doesn't know why whales exhibit this behavior. Scientists have theories about why they breach: to communicate, attract other whales, or warn off other males.

But no one knows why—yet.

Well, how about this as a theory:

What if they're jumping for joy?

Maybe all creation has its unique way of practicing gratitude and praising God. Maybe that's why whales breach, fireflies glow, and swallows whoosh and whirl playfully in the air. Maybe we were made for it.

And maybe that's why we feel unbalanced when we aren't doing it and better when we do. It is just a theory, but a bestselling book proclaims, "Let the sea resound, and all that is in it . . . Let all creation rejoice before the Lord."

When we focus on the stuff that's missing from our stories, it's the equivalent of inviting Adultitis into your living room and encouraging him to put up his feet while you prepare him a seven-course dinner. That's fine if you want to do that, but you shouldn't be surprised at how difficult it is to get him to leave at the end of the night.

On the other hand, cultivating a sense of gratitude is like slapping a restraining order on the big jerk.

It seems ironic to turn to gratitude in times of anxiety, grief, or pain. But gratitude is a discipline. We typically want to feel it before having it, but oftentimes, feelings don't precede an action. We usually reserve "jumping for joy" for when we feel good about something remarkable.

The truth is, something remarkable is always happening.

You are already living a charmed life. Praise aligns us with our Creator, giving us the new eyes we need to see it.

When my family and I lived in Madison, Wisconsin, there was a large, wooded marsh with a network of winding trails near our house. Just about every day, either Kim or I or both of us were out taking a walk in that marsh.

One day I stumbled upon three deer. We all froze. I bet I spent five minutes standing there, quietly, having a staring contest with them. When they finally bounded off like NFL wide receivers, I marveled at their grace and power.

I love those encounters.

And I am grateful for that marsh.

Interestingly, it wasn't one of the listed selling points when we bought that house. We didn't even know it existed until months after we moved in. But when we left that home for our next adventure, the marsh was one of the hardest things to let go.

Everyone knows that if you plan well and work hard, good things usually happen. But I'm sure we'd all agree that we have many blessings in our lives we didn't plan for, orchestrate, or, frankly, don't even deserve.

It's worth taking some time every now and then to reflect on those "undeserved" blessings in order to invite a sense of gratitude to envelop us. It's also an undisputed way to turn frowns upside down.

Our lists will look different, of course, but that marsh would definitely be on mine. Along with the parents I was lucky enough to be born to. And the talents I was somehow gifted. And the strangers who crossed my path that eventually became friends and mentors. Not to mention the blonde girl I met over twenty-five years ago who saw something in me and turned into the best wife and partner-in-crime a guy could ever ask for.

I didn't orchestrate any of those things, but boy, am I ever grateful for them.

Maybe it's easier to look for reasons to panic, pout, and pontificate about how life stinks. But it's more useful and uplifting to search for the good things we did nothing to earn and rejoice over just how blessed we really are.

I hope that you already have a healthy list of must be nices rolling around in your noggin. If so, let's make it even longer. If not, let's do something to change that!

It turns out the best way to assemble a big list of must be nices is to start by writing down things you're grateful for, including the things you did nothing to earn.

Can you come up with fifty? Of course you can! Let's go!

" **Reflect upon your present blessings—of which every man has many—not on your past misfortunes, of which all men have some.** "

—Charles Dickens

50 Things I'm Grateful For

1. I overcame 1 in 400 quadrillion odds
   to be born. *(Must be nice.)*

2. I have the impeccable taste and good
   sense to read this book. *(Must be nice.)*

3. _____
   _____ *(Must be nice.)*

4. _____
   _____ *(Must be nice.)*

5. _____
   _____ *(Must be nice.)*

6. _____
   _____ *(Must be nice.)*

7. _____
   _____ *(Must be nice.)*

8. _____
   _____ *(Must be nice.)*

> "He is a wise man who does not grieve for the things which he has not, but rejoices for those which he has."

—Epictetus

9. _____
_____ (Must be nice.)

10. _____
_____ (Must be nice.)

11. _____
_____ (Must be nice.)

12. _____
_____ (Must be nice.)

13. _____
_____ (Must be nice.)

14. _____
_____ (Must be nice.)

15. _____
_____ (Must be nice.)

16. _____
_____ (Must be nice.)

17. _____
_____ (Must be nice.)

" Piglet noticed that even though he had a Very Small Heart, it could hold a rather large amount of Gratitude. "

—A.A. Miline

18. _____
_____ (Must be nice.)

19. _____
_____ (Must be nice.)

20. _____
_____ (Must be nice.)

21. _____
_____ (Must be nice.)

22. _____
_____ (Must be nice.)

23. _____
_____ (Must be nice.)

24. _____
_____ (Must be nice.)

25. _____
_____ (Must be nice.)

26. _____
_____ (Must be nice.)

"Gratitude is riches.
Complaint is poverty.

—Doris Day

27. _____
(Must be nice.)

28. _____
(Must be nice.)

29. _____
(Must be nice.)

30. _____
(Must be nice.)

31. _____
(Must be nice.)

32. _____
(Must be nice.)

33. _____
(Must be nice.)

34. _____
(Must be nice.)

35. _____
(Must be nice.)

" We often take for granted the very things that most deserve our gratitude. "

—Cynthia Ozick

36. _____
   _____ (Must be nice.)

37. _____
   _____ (Must be nice.)

38. _____
   _____ (Must be nice.)

39. _____
   _____ (Must be nice.)

40. _____
   _____ (Must be nice.)

41. _____
   _____ (Must be nice.)

42. _____
   _____ (Must be nice.)

43. _____
   _____ (Must be nice.)

44. _____
   _____ (Must be nice.)

"Enjoy the little things, for one day you may look back and realize they were the big things."

—Robert Brault

45. _____
   _____ (Must be nice.)

46. _____
   _____ (Must be nice.)

47. _____
   _____ (Must be nice.)

48. _____
   _____ (Must be nice.)

49. _____
   _____ (Must be nice.)

50. _____
   _____ (Must be nice.)

"I don't even have any good skills. You know, like nunchuck skills, bow hunting skills, computer hacking skills. Girls only want boyfriends who have great skills!"

—Napoleon Dynamite

IKEA instructions give me the cold sweats.

My dad was a carpenter, but I am not the least bit handy, unless you want me to screw in a lightbulb or put a nail in a wall to hang a photo. It took me an hour to figure out how to change the spark plug in my lawnmower last summer. Since we're on the subject of personal deficiencies, I also cannot solve even the most remedial algebra equation. And I am terrible at remembering names.

On the other hand, I am a talented artist. An excellent speaker. A really good writer. Handy in the kitchen, too.

Even though there are people who wish they were half as good as me at the things I do well, I bemoan the areas of my life where I am below average and beat myself up for not being better at the things I stink at. Can you relate?

I blame the report card.

In the traditional education system, the report card is a record of our proficiency in a wide variety of subjects: math, science, language, history, physical fitness, etc. And what's the ideal? Straight As. We are ranked according to grade point average, and the only path to the top is being awesome at everything.

The downfall of this scenario is that if someone passes English with flying colors but performs poorly in math, we're liable to brand them as deficient and stick them in a remedial class.

Imagine: Beethoven can't pass a spelling test so we label him as one of the dumb kids.

From our earliest days, the report card makes it clear that success looks like being good at everything. Anything less is frowned upon. Is it any wonder why people apologize when they're not an expert after trying something for the first time?

Spoiler alert: people who get straight As are not actually good at everything. I should know because my report card was often filled with them. The only definitive thing straight As tells you is that you were good at . . . school.

Being good at school requires a different skill set than winning at life.

This subconscious programming by our educational system is a severe detriment to our ability and willingness to tinker. Not only does it limit our future growth, but it's also not at all reflective of what we encounter in the real world.

In the real world, we are rewarded for what we do well, not for being well-rounded.

LeBron James does one thing really, really well and is richly rewarded for it. I'm not sure if he ever passed trigonometry.

Let's not argue that we place too much value on tossing an orange ball through a circle with a net for a dress—I tend to agree—because the premise still stands:

Do you care if the dentist doing your root canal got a D in history?*

Do you care if the chef at your favorite restaurant aced geography?

When your kitchen is flooding, do you care if your plumber has always struggled to understand what the hell Shakespeare was talking about?

Please hear me. You not being good at everything doesn't make you broken. Or not enough. **It makes you human.**

I was talking to my dentist about this the other day, and she admitted that she couldn't carry a tune to save her life, even though her mom had sung the national anthem at a Milwaukee Brewers game. "It's amazing that they still let you be a dentist," I joked.

Believe it or not, you're actually better than Einstein.

I read once that Albert Einstein didn't know how to swim. And he was a terrible sailor, capsizing his boat so often that locals regularly had to tow him back to shore.

It made me feel good to read that.

I have never sailed, but I do know how to swim. It's nice to know that I can do something Einstein couldn't, and that he stunk at things.

As I shared previously, I spend too much time worrying that I'm not enough. I'm not outgoing enough, smart enough, creative enough, disciplined enough, thin enough, or faithful enough to accomplish my biggest dreams. I regularly undervalue my gifts and overemphasize my shortcomings.

Maybe you do the same thing.

We regularly compare ourselves to people like Einstein, who is lauded as a genius, and cast ourselves in lesser roles in this grand production called life.

Interestingly, our definition of genius has changed over the years. In the fourteenth century, a genius referred to a guardian spirit, and a very talented person was said to "have" a genius because his or her gift was thought to be the result of some supernatural help.

Somewhere along the line, we evolved from the idea of having a genius to being one, which brings with it the connotation of being superhuman and great at everything.

But no one is great at everything. No one is even great at most things. We weren't designed to be all-powerful, self-sufficient beings. We were designed to need one another. For instance, I get paid to give a speech that encourages a team of employees at a company, and I use the money to pay a plumber to fix my sink's leaky pipe. We are made to work together, and we all have a part to play.

A person cannot make a baby alone.

Babies can't change their own diapers.

And diaper companies can't make money without babies.

Despite finding himself regularly waterlogged, Einstein apparently didn't think it was important enough to invest any time in becoming a better sailor or learning how to swim.

I'm guessing he also didn't waste any time comparing himself to Johnny Weissmuller.

If you haven't heard of Johnny Weissmuller, he lived at the same time as Einstein, and he sure could swim. He won three gold medals at the 1924 Summer Olympics, three years after Einstein won the Nobel Prize in Physics. Weissmuller also became the best-known actor to play Tarzan in films of the 1930s and 1940s. (His character's distinctive Tarzan yell is still often used in films.) He had a different kind of genius than old Albert.

Weissmuller's Wikipedia page doesn't mention whether Johnny was any good at math or science.

But he was way better than Einstein at swimming.

You're better than Einstein at something, too. We all have a genius. We're all pretty good at something. (At least sixty-four somethings, probably, but more on that soon.) That's our genius, and that's what we need to share with the world.

Your job is to combine the handful of things you're pretty good at and let them shine in a way only you can.

Develop and share your genius.

Disregard the things you stink at.

Even Einstein wasn't an Einstein at everything.

Ah, the sixty-four box of Crayola crayons.

Was there anything that made you feel more like a millionaire when you were a kid than having a fresh box of sixty-four crayons, all with sharp tips and a built-in sharpener guaranteed to keep them that way?

A box of eight was utilitarian, a box of twenty-four was nice, and a box of forty-eight was pretty awesome, like a big house in the suburbs. But there was something about that box of sixty-four that tickled the imagination. It felt as if you had access to every color God had ever invented.

The possibilities were endless.

goldenrod
amarillo oro

cornflower
azul aciano
bleuet

bittersweet
agridulce
douce-amère

sea green
verde mar
vert marin

brick red
rojo ladrillo
rouge brique

periwinkle
florecita azul claro
pervenche

124

Of course, they have changed the colors over the years, but anyone of a certain age will remember these classics:

Goldenrod

Cornflower

Bittersweet

Sea green

Brick red

And don't forget periwinkle.

Then factor in silver and gold—which you assumed were made with real bits of the precious metals—c'mon! You were living the high life!

If you possessed a box of sixty-four, there was no reason for debate. You were an artist. You had limitless potential. There was nothing you couldn't handle, what with yellow-green and green-yellow at your disposal.

I believe we are still artists, whether or not a stick figure is the peak of your drawing abilities.

We are all here to make the world more beautiful by creating masterpieces of our lives. Our talents, gifts, and must be nices are our tools, like crayons in a box. Believe it or not, you have at least sixty-four of them. Yours are different than mine, but you have more than enough to whip up something worth hanging on the fridge.

You might not believe me. That might be because you're ruined by the classic question heard at every cocktail party and networking event: "So, what do you do?"

As if your life can be narrowed down to one thing. (Pro tip: you can be more than one thing.)

Life is better when you have access to all the colors.

Don't get me wrong. I'm not suggesting there are sixty-four things that you are the best in the world at, or even the best at in your town. News flash: you're probably not the best in the world at anything. Who cares?

this isn't a competition.

it's a community service project.

What I am suggesting is that you have at least sixty-four things you're pretty good at.

Pretty good is a pretty low bar, if you think about it.

But we can accomplish something with pretty good.

For instance, sure, I'm a gifted artist, writer, and public speaker. But I'm also pretty good at creating systems. I'm pretty good at navigating new places. Pretty good at noticing things most people miss. Pretty good at making homemade pasta. Pretty good at asking questions. Pretty good at listening. Pretty good at tying cherry stems with my tongue.

As you can see, a small fraction of those things contribute to my income. But that doesn't mean they're not valuable. And in case you haven't figured it out, all those things I'm pretty good at are a must be nice for someone else. (Did you say that for any of the things on my list? Be honest!)

You have your own list of sixty-four things you're pretty good at. As I mentioned earlier, your unique superpowers are often hiding in what comes easy to you and what you geek out on. As someone who requires a personal tour guide at Home Depot, being able to make a table out of wood—without a pictogram from a Swedish furniture company—is a big deal.

I invite you to add to your list of must be nices by recording sixty-four things you're pretty good at.

I'm not gonna lie—coming up with sixty-four things is hard. It might be uncomfortable or feel prideful. But this is not about bragging. This is about identifying all the ways you're able to make the world a better place for the rest of us, including the people you care about most. A great way to begin is by asking yourself the following questions:

What comes easy to me?

What do I love doing?

You could also ask a friend, *"What am I good at?"* to identify skills you take for granted.

It might take a while, but you should be able to get to sixty-four.

Finally, here's a huge cheat sheet of additional ideas to get your brain rolling. Steal them if they fit. Let them inspire you to think of more.

I know how to: smile. sew. knit. crochet. code. design. draw. cook. bake. brew craft beer. write a thank-you note. write a grant proposal. troubleshoot computers. do taxes. ride a horse. ride a motorcycle. change the oil in my car. change a tire. play an instrument. cut hair. type. give hugs. play chess. speak Spanish. speak Chinese. juggle. weld. roller-skate.

I am good at: organizing. gardening. singing. dancing. creating contingency plans/floor plans/game plans. telling stories. fixing things. math. making spreadsheets. scrapbooking. drawing. selling. marketing. listening. naming that tune. interior decorating. finding answers. finding good deals. giving advice. anticipating potential problems. brainstorming. running. planning. lifting heavy things. noticing the talents of others. making complex things simple. playing cards. throwing parties. planning trips. telling jokes. solving puzzles. proofreading. decorating cakes. being silly. speaking in public. calculating probabilities. photography. troubleshooting. asking questions. networking. negotiating. teaching.

I have: a good sense of humor. a calming voice. a bold voice. a distinct voice. a photographic memory. a surplus of money. a lot of energy. an extra bedroom. a few hours a week. plenty of food. a willingness to help. frequent flyer miles. wisdom to share. a kind heart. experience. more clothes than I need. my health.

**What are the
tasks I do well
at work?**

64 Things I'm Pretty Good At

1. *I can read.* (Must be nice.)

2. _____
   _____ (Must be nice.)

3. _____
   _____ (Must be nice.)

4. _____
   _____ (Must be nice.)

5. _____
   _____ (Must be nice.)

6. _____
   _____ (Must be nice.)

7. _____
   _____ (Must be nice.)

8. _____
   _____ (Must be nice.)

What things did I do well as a kid (even if I haven't done them in thirty years)?

9. _____
_____ (Must be nice.)

10. _____
_____ (Must be nice.)

11. _____
_____ (Must be nice.)

12. _____
_____ (Must be nice.)

13. _____
_____ (Must be nice.)

14. _____
_____ (Must be nice.)

15. _____
_____ (Must be nice.)

16. _____
_____ (Must be nice.)

17. _____
_____ (Must be nice.)

What are other people always asking me to do for them?

18. _____
(Must be nice.)
_____

19. _____
(Must be nice.)
_____

20. _____
(Must be nice.)
_____

21. _____
(Must be nice.)
_____

22. _____
(Must be nice.)
_____

23. _____
(Must be nice.)
_____

24. _____
(Must be nice.)
_____

25. _____
(Must be nice.)
_____

26. _____
(Must be nice.)
_____

What are
the things I've
loved doing since
childhood?

27. _____
_____ (Must be nice.)

28. _____
_____ (Must be nice.)

29. _____
_____ (Must be nice.)

30. _____
_____ (Must be nice.)

31. _____
_____ (Must be nice.)

32. _____
_____ (Must be nice.)

33. _____
_____ (Must be nice.)

34. _____
_____ (Must be nice.)

35. _____
_____ (Must be nice.)

What minor or obscure skills do I possess?

36. _____

(Must be nice.)

37. _____

(Must be nice.)

38. _____

(Must be nice.)

39. _____

(Must be nice.)

40. _____

(Must be nice.)

41. _____

(Must be nice.)

42. _____

(Must be nice.)

43. _____

(Must be nice.)

44. _____

(Must be nice.)

What is something I'm better at than the three people I'm closest to?

45. _____
   _____ (Must be nice.)
46. _____
   _____ (Must be nice.)
47. _____
   _____ (Must be nice.)
48. _____
   _____ (Must be nice.)
49. _____
   _____ (Must be nice.)
50. _____
   _____ (Must be nice.)
51. _____
   _____ (Must be nice.)
52. _____
   _____ (Must be nice.)
53. _____
   _____ (Must be nice.)

What was I
the best at in
my family?

54. _____
     (Must be nice.)
55. _____
     (Must be nice.)
56. _____
     (Must be nice.)

This is hard, right?

You've got this.

These last few are not only the most difficult to tease
out but also the most valuable and insightful.

What do people compliment me for?

57. _____
   _____ (Must be nice.)
58. _____
   _____ (Must be nice.)
59. _____
   _____ (Must be nice.)
60. _____
   _____ (Must be nice.)
61. _____
   _____ (Must be nice.)
62. _____
   _____ (Must be nice.)
63. _____
   _____ (Must be nice.)
64. _____
   _____ (Must be nice.)

Part 3: How to Leverage Your Must Be Nice

LUCKY
Girl

When we started homeschooling our kids, Kim and I attended conferences to borrow courage and learn from people who were already doing it. Most families had one person who worked a typical job as the primary breadwinner, while the other person stayed home and assumed the lion's share of the homeschooling efforts. Their family travel was limited by how much vacation time the working spouse had available. It didn't take long to realize how lucky we were to own our own business and that said business not only had so much travel built in but that a lot of it was paid for by a speaking client. It was a gargantuan must be nice, to say the least.

It was a huge revelation—"That's one hell of a must be nice!"—followed by an important question: "Are you taking advantage of it?"

I can assure you that since then, we have.

The entire reason I wrote this book is to help you quit wishing for someone else's must be nices, figure out what yours are, and make the most of them.

And that last part might be the most important part.

It's one thing to stop wishing for someone else's gold coin.

It's another to find the gold coin in your own pocket.

Lucky
Guy

But things really get good when you figure out how to spend it.

My art talent is a gargantuan must be nice, but my career didn't take off until I started incorporating it into my speaking business.

My speaker colleagues hate me because my wife shares my passion for fighting Adultitis and books all my gigs and travel. Must be nice, huh?

You're damn right it is!

I'm not a former NBA player, a Fortune 100 CEO, or a good juggler. But you better believe we use Kim's world-class skills of connecting with clients and managing travel details to our benefit.

Your job is to not only identify your must be nices but leverage them. One way to do that is by combining them.

I don't know about you, but the list of things I'm not so good at is way longer than the list of things I'm pretty good at. But guess what? That doesn't nullify or remove anything on the pretty good list.

153

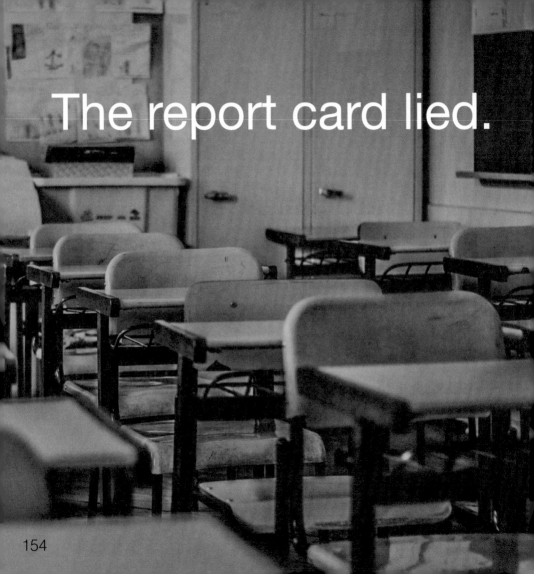

The report card lied.

Getting straight As is not the best indicator for success in life.

You don't have to be great at everything. You don't have to be an Einstein or a LeBron James of anything.

Yes, it is possible to achieve success by specializing in one thing. We might see this in sports—see LeBron—as well as medicine, mathematics, and acting. This path is extremely difficult.

But besides being world class in one area, you can also become valuable by combining ordinary but complementary skills that help you stand out and achieve great success. In fact, this is the most common and accessible path.

The trick is to follow the advice of Kevin Kelly, who shares in his book *Excellent Advice for Living:* "Don't be the best. Be the only."

It may sound daunting, but you can do this by assembling a talent stack.

Scott Adams, the creator of the comic strip *Dilbert*, popularized this concept which states that all you have to do to ensure success is assemble a "stack" of two or more complementary skills and be in the top 25 percent or so in each. Do that and you'll be unstoppable.

In his case, he readily admits he's not the best artist, the most skilled writer, or the savviest business expert. But his unique combination of those skill sets has contributed to his success as a cartoonist. Adams says, "The magic is that few people can draw well and write jokes. It's the combination of the two that makes what I do so rare. And when you add in my business background, suddenly I had a topic that few cartoonists could hope to understand without living it. When you add in my ordinary business skills, my strong work ethic, my risk tolerance, and my reasonably good sense of humor, I'm fairly unique. And in this case that uniqueness has commercial value."

My talent stack began with a few crayons, I'd guess. I don't know for sure because I've been drawing for as long as I can remember, and my memory gets a little fuzzy when I dig that far into the archives. I've always enjoyed it, and I got praised for it, so I'm sure that made me want to keep doing it. "Artist" was my first and is my longest-lasting identity.

158

In school, I always liked English class and expressing my creativity through words. In high school, I had a chance to take a creative writing class, which I enjoyed exponentially more than any of my math classes. I kept honing that skill, and it eventually became an indispensable part of my talent stack.

In college, I gave a talk as a leader on a retreat and received great reviews. I had taken a speech class in high school but only earned a C (which is notable given that my report card was mostly filled with As). Turns out that talking about something that mattered to me and seeing how it could impact the lives of the people I shared it with was a game changer.

Even though I have been shy and not at all a showman or someone hungry for the spotlight, I enjoyed the creative process of crafting stories in spoken form. It was like creative writing but delivered out loud.

To the surprise of me, my parents, and my high school speech teacher, public speaking emerged as the primary driver of our business. I went from giving cartooning workshops in schools to speaking at churches to keynoting conferences for associations and corporations all over the place.

It took me a few years to realize that these three talents—art, writing, and speaking—are not separate skills that operate independently but are part of a talent stack, that when used in harmony become powerful. We all know artists. But not many of them are eager to stand on a stage in front of a thousand people to give a talk. That's unique. And my writing is the foundation of all of it, from the books I write to the stories I tell on stage.

I am not the best artist in the world, or the best writer or speaker. But I'm pretty good at all three, and that combination has been the secret sauce of my success.

Once I discovered the idea of a talent stack, I have eagerly looked for complementary skills to add to it. By devouring hundreds of marketing books and through the school of trial and error, I have achieved the equivalent of an MBA in marketing. Am I the best marketer in the world? No, but I easily fall into the top 25 percent.

Kim and I went on several organized retreats in high school and college. That background gave us a foundation to build on when we started hosting our own events. After putting on numerous meetups, workshops, book tours, fundraising galas, and Escape Adulthood Summits over the past two decades, we've gotten pretty good at managing logistics and creating experiences that move people.

At the onset of the COVID-19 pandemic, when all our in-person speaking gigs went up in smoke, Kim and I turned on the video camera. We went live to our tribe for twenty-eight straight days to offer encouragement and hope. Our first efforts were from the heart but woefully subpar on a technical level. But each day, we tinkered with something. I tried a new lighting technique. Upgraded the microphone. Installed new software. Bought a new camera. Incorporated sound effects. We played with different types of segments and ways of adding interactivity, paying attention to what resonated with viewers.

Eventually, we turned our daily kitchen table chats into a weekly show, which opened the doors to delivering virtual presentations and earning tens of thousands of dollars producing a video series for global corporations from the comfort of our basement.

Drip by drip, these new skills, fueled by my interests and talents, have helped make the other skills even more valuable.

I share all this to illustrate how a talent stack can take shape over the course of a life. Your talent stack will look different from mine, but the premise is the same. Start with natural strengths and abilities and work to make them better. Think about how they can work together in unexpected ways, even if they seem unrelated.

The glue in your stack that enhances your originality will be traits that come naturally to you; not necessarily "talents" but personality strengths. Think of the charisma of Dwayne Johnson, the gentleness of Fred Rogers, the empathy of Oprah Winfrey, the imagination of Dr. Seuss. They aren't things you can manufacture, but they flavor the skills and areas of expertise you can develop. This personality element is a multiplier that enhances your talent stack and distinguishes you from those who have similar skills.

Here is a simplistic formula to illustrate how it looks:

Muscle-building skills **+** entertainment skills **+** speaking skills **x** charisma **=** Dwayne Johnson

Psychology skills **+** puppetry skills **+** television skills **x** gentleness **=** Mr. Rogers

Television skills **+** interviewing skills **+** business skills **x** empathy **=** Oprah

Drawing skills **+** linguistic skills **+** humor skills **x** imagination **=** Dr. Seuss

Since I was a kid, I have been sensitive and introspective. My art, writing, and speaking talents are influenced by my personality in a way that would be different if I were more gregarious and extroverted.

If you are struggling to think of your current talent stack as anything more substantial than a lonely pancake on an oversized plate, I'd invite you to revisit the activities earlier in the book. Within your list of over a hundred must be nices are a plethora of clues.

If you are in a competitive field, everyone in your industry probably competes on many of the same skills. What do you have that's different? Oftentimes the magic lies in an unrelated skill or an interest that seems to come out of left field. For instance, many professional speakers are also writers. But my artistic gifts and whimsical, childlike perspective toward life help me offer something extraordinary.

Consciously look for other skills you might be able to attain that complement and enrich the others. This isn't just about what you were born with. What one or two skills could you add that would help you stand out? That might involve a traditional degree or certification, but it can also be done by reading books, listening to podcasts from industry experts, taking courses online or at your local community college, or practicing, in public, every day, like we did with our pandemic project of livestreaming.

If you're stuck, here are some evergreen choices that will help:

Presentation skills

Technology skills

Foreign language skills

Sales or marketing skills

Writing skills

Business management skills

Nunchuck skills...

Remember, you don't have to turn yourself into the foremost expert on any of these skills. Just be in the top 25 percent. Said another way, in a world of around eight billion people, you only need to be among the top two billion. If one hundred thousand people live in your city, you just have to be in the top twenty-five thousand.

In other words, **pretty good** is good enough.

Keep in mind that this is a lifelong
project. If you're doing it right—meaning
you stay curious and keep growing—your
talent stack will continue to evolve and strengthen
throughout your career and life.

When you have a decent stack of three to five skills going, you
can bank on someone, somewhere observing what you've
been able to accomplish and saying, "Must be nice."

Once your talent stack starts taking shape,
it's time to think **bigger.**

Are you Hall of Fame material?

Go ahead, think about it. **Are you?**

While you're mulling that over, let me ask you another question: Did you know that there is a National Toy Hall of Fame? It's true. Housed at the Strong National Museum of Play in Rochester, NY, it honors classics like Lincoln Logs, the Hula-Hoop, the Slinky, and even the multi-talented cardboard box. What makes a toy Hall of Fame worthy? Well, it turns out there are four official selection criteria:

1 Icon status. The toy is widely recognized, respected, and remembered.

2 Longevity. The toy is more than a passing fad and has enjoyed popularity over multiple generations.

3 Discovery. The toy fosters learning, creativity, or discovery through play.

4 Innovation. The toy profoundly changed play or toy design. A toy may be inducted based on this criterion without necessarily having met all of the first three.

Undoubtedly, Lincoln Logs clear all four hurdles. But what about us? We're not toys. What, if anything, can people learn about greatness from Hall of Fame–caliber toys? Quite a bit, actually. The four criteria can be helpful in measuring our greatness as well.

icon status

Let's start with icon status. When your time on Earth is over, will you be widely recognized, respected, and remembered? Keep in mind we're not talking about fame here. I know teachers who are beloved icons in the middle schools where they teach, even though they may be completely unknown a few school districts over.

longevity

What about longevity? Anybody can have a good day, a good week, or even a good year. The greats show up year after year. They are persistent, consistent, and stand the test of time. Are you in it for the long haul?

discovery

Discovery, as it is used here, can be summed up in one word: empowerment. You can build a million things with Lincoln Logs. That's what makes them great: they jump-start the imagination of the players themselves. Likewise, we are great when we empower others to be great.

innovation

What's interesting about innovation is that it's such a big deal that a toy can get in based on innovation alone, even if it doesn't meet the other three criteria. This is because it's so hard to do.

Innovation is rare, but not because it's unreachable. You have the potential to profoundly change the world you live in. But doing so requires immense courage and bravery. You have to be willing to challenge conventional wisdom, buck the status quo, and take a stand without any guarantee that anyone will follow you. (Most likely, they won't, at least at first.)

Back to the
question about you
being Hall of Fame
material.

Are you?

The answer is **YES.**

kotecki

SPEONK LUMBER and SUPPLY Co.

A million times yes. You are.

Don't be fooled by the fact that there probably isn't an actual Hall of Fame in your area of giftedness. That doesn't disqualify you from being one of the all-time greats. What would it take to be a Hall of Fame teacher? Nurse? Team leader? Cub Scout leader? Janitor? Mom? Grandparent? Snow plow driver?

Refuse to settle for average. Regardless of what you believe or may have been taught, the seeds of greatness are within you. Your family, your colleagues, and your community need you to share that greatness.

How?

Let the Lincoln Log be your guide.

But let's not stop at

the Hall of Fame . . .

How many
Super Bowl
rings does
it take to
become a
goat?

the GReAtEST
OF all time

kolecki

I am not referring to those four-legged, cheese-making mammals with a taste for tin cans.

I'm talking about the label of GOAT—**the greatest of all time.**

With more than two decades in the NFL, more touchdown passes than any other quarterback, and more Super Bowl rings than anyone in history, Tom Brady is widely regarded as the GOAT, at least when it comes to quarterbacks.

Frankly, I'm still getting used to being labeled a "goat" as a good thing. In 1986, Bill Buckner was called a goat for letting an easy ground ball roll past him in a World Series game, and it definitely wasn't meant as a compliment. (Ah, the ever-present thin line between hero and villain.)

Debating the greatest of all time is a juicy topic for sports talk radio, but what makes the discussion so compelling? Why such an obsession with greatness?

Besides the fact that we like comparing things (and arguing!), greatness stirs something within us. We are inspired when we see it manifested, be it in the long and decorated career of Tom Brady or in the gold medal performance of figure skater Nathan Chen.

But greatness stretches far beyond the sports world:

We see it in a delicious dish prepared with ease by Gordon Ramsay.

We saw it in the remarkable daring and bravery of Amelia Earhart.

We saw it in the spellbinding gentleness and kindness of Fred Rogers.

We saw it in the compelling selflessness and compassion of Mother Teresa.

The greatness of these individuals is so profound and self-evident, it's easy to assume they are rare geniuses who possess mystical talents. Their level of excellence appears unattainable for us mere mortals. Their talent is unmistakable, and they "have a genius," but the individuals we place on the pedestal of greatness are merely human beings whose extraordinary results came from the consistent practice of ordinary things.

Our preoccupation with debating the greatest of all time is a trap that prevents us from striving for greatness ourselves.

It's easier to argue about the top five saints of all time than aim to become one.

I've already made the case that you have Hall of Fame potential. *Am I now suggesting you are GOAT material?*

Actually, yes.

Hear me out. Usually, the title of GOAT is bestowed on someone famous, known for their professional accomplishments, and often in a domain conducive to measurable outcomes.

But what about people who aren't famous? Isn't it possible that some Inca woman possessed unmatched skill as a potter with her only flaw being born at a time when she couldn't have her own YouTube channel?

And what if your skill is not as esteemed or public as that of a professional athlete or celebrity chef? Could an unknown Amish grandmother technically be the greatest bread maker of all time? And tell me, who is the greatest school custodian of all time? The greatest dental hygienist of all time? The greatest administrative assistant of all time?

What about domains lacking metrics that are easy to quantify? When it comes to football, we can compare wins, passing yards, touchdowns, longevity, playoff appearances, awards, and Super Bowl rings, all while debating the relative importance of each. But how would one go about naming the Greatest Mother of All Time? The Greatest Father of All Time? The Greatest Wife or Husband or Friend or Next-Door Neighbor of All Time?

Most of us don't have trading cards with our pictures on them, and if we did, they wouldn't have stats on the back totaling Boo-Boos Kissed, Lunches Prepared, Loads of Laundry Completed, Encouraging Words Spoken, or Hugs Delivered.

Without these metrics a Google search away, what would it take for **YOU** to become the GOAT?

193

If you're normal, you might be thinking, *Slow your roll, buddy. I already feel like I'm falling short, day after day. I barely qualify as a good parent, let alone the GOAT.*

I hear you. Sometimes I feel like I'm leading the league in dropped balls.

The good news is that the seeds of greatness are in our DNA because we each have a spark of the divine within us.

Simply put, you were born for greatness.

Don't let my famous examples fool you. One dictionary defines great as "remarkable in magnitude, quality, skill, or effectiveness." The steps to achieving greatness are accessible to everyone. Including me. And you. The steps are simple, but not easy.

Identify your gifts.

We've already spent time uncovering your gifts. These are your raw materials for greatness. And remember, "better than everyone else in the world" at anything is not a requirement for greatness.

Honor your gifts.

If you treasure a gift, you don't take it for granted or throw it in a corner. To give your gifts the respect they deserve, use them, share them, and work to improve them. Deliberately build your talent stack. Shoring up weaknesses can be helpful, but keep in mind that Mister Rogers wasn't as bold and gregarious as Gordon Ramsay, who was not as gentle or vulnerable as Mister Rogers. Their must be nices are different. Greatness lies in maximizing your strengths.

Be committed.

Greatness requires the willingness to do what no one else will. Not many are willing to stick to the diet and workout routine that helped Tom Brady stay so productive for so long. Even fewer are clamoring to comfort the sick and clean the sores of people living in the slums of Calcutta, as Mother Teresa did. Amelia Earhart was willing to attempt dangerous things no one else had ever done, consequences be damned.

Keep going.

Nathan Chen's debut Olympic performance was a disaster, riddled with falls. Gordon Ramsay didn't make a perfect omelet on his first try. Tom Brady didn't win every playoff game he was in. The great ones aren't people who never get knocked down. They're the ones who keep getting up when they do.

Empower others.

Through his example alone, Fred Rogers inspired millions of people—most who had never met him—to treat others with more respect and kindness than they might have otherwise. Tom Brady's drive, high standards, and work ethic empowered his teammates to be better. Mother Teresa built a community of sisters who followed her lead and carried on her work after she was gone. Your own humble journey toward greatness may be your most enduring legacy.

You might not ever be inducted into a Hall of Fame. It's unlikely that you or I will ever be publicly regarded as the GOAT of anything. Unless you're Muhammad Ali—"I am the greatest!"—the title is bestowed on you by others. We can't control it. Who cares?

When it comes to greatness, everyone else is irrelevant. There is one category you can be assured of being the GOAT in, and that's the category of you.

your job
is to be the
greatest
YOU
of all time

If you learned a new thing today or did something to improve your craft or make yourself better than you were yesterday, congrats. You are officially the greatest you of all time.

If you got up today after being knocked down yesterday, your legend just gained a new comeback story and you're officially the greatest you of all time.

If you used one of your gifts to make someone's day or lessen the burden of another soul, your scoreboard of contributions to the world just increased by one, officially making you the greatest you of all time.

Instead of wasting our time arguing over who is the GOAT, may we use their example as inspiration to cultivate our own greatness within us.

Identify your gifts. Honor them by honing them and sharing them with others. Be committed. Keep going. And empower others along the way.

We can't count on being considered the greatest. But that doesn't mean we shouldn't strive to be great.

Regardless of whether you play in the NFL or make soufflés on TV, those principles are controllable. If you practice them, I can't guarantee you'll ever be deemed the GOAT by pundits, historians, or late-night callers on talk radio.

But I will guarantee that people will be inspired by the greatness they see within you. No Super Bowl rings required.

Conclusion

I was sitting in the backyard, reading a book, enjoying the fine summer day. All was calm. Out of nowhere appeared a whirling dervish of purple and teal. My youngest daughter came zipping around the corner on her bike, sporting an oversized helmet and a big, toothy smile. The sun illuminated her light hair, making it look like a halo on fire in the golden sun. Saying not a word, she pedaled through the grass like she was on a mission—and I've no doubt she was—but with a look of contentment as if she had not one care in the world.

And then, just like that, she was g o n e.

The moment lasted all of seven seconds, but it was the one that came to mind that night, as I lay in bed thinking about my happiest moment from the day. I've adopted the routine of falling asleep contemplating the day's happiest moment. It's a good practice in gratitude, it's easy to do, and it beats falling to sleep worrying about all the undone things waiting for me when I wake up.

It's helped me see that even though we spend so much of our lives pursuing happiness, sometimes it streaks by us unexpectedly, in seven-second bursts.

It often feels like my life is oriented around making lists of things that need to be done. These lists almost never contain what will end up being my happiest moment of the day.

My happiest moments are rarely the "important" accomplishments of the day. They are small moments, like a lakeside walk with Kim, or waking up to six deer using our backyard for their living room, peacefully lounging about with their backs coated in snow.

Or watching Lucy ride her newly leased horse Chester, with the excitement of a beginner and the confidence of a pro.

Or seeing the joy on Ben's face after catching his fifth pop-up in a row.

Or the spontaneous conversation that bubbled up with Ginny while we were sitting on the Healing Swing, when we talked about Wisconsin birds and calculated how many of her is the deepest part of Lake Michigan. (It's about 230 Ginnys deep, in case you're wondering.)

moments

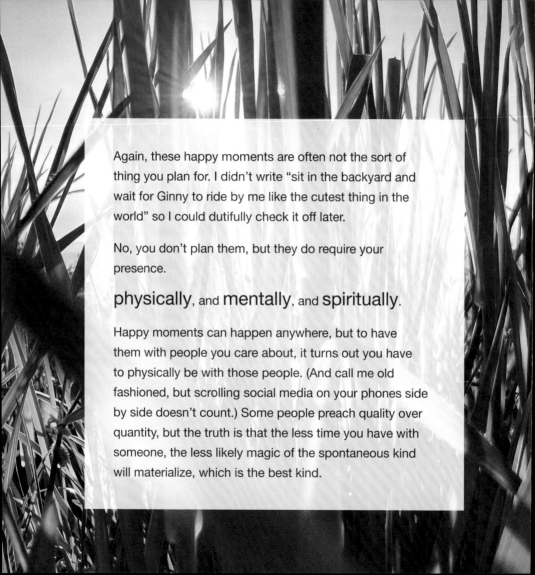

Again, these happy moments are often not the sort of thing you plan for. I didn't write "sit in the backyard and wait for Ginny to ride by me like the cutest thing in the world" so I could dutifully check it off later.

No, you don't plan them, but they do require your presence.

physically, and mentally, and spiritually.

Happy moments can happen anywhere, but to have them with people you care about, it turns out you have to physically be with those people. (And call me old fashioned, but scrolling social media on your phones side by side doesn't count.) Some people preach quality over quantity, but the truth is that the less time you have with someone, the less likely magic of the spontaneous kind will materialize, which is the best kind.

How much time are you spending with the people you love most?

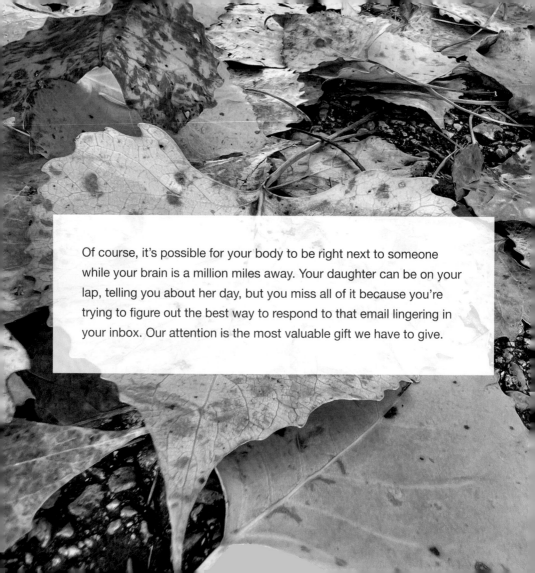

Of course, it's possible for your body to be right next to someone while your brain is a million miles away. Your daughter can be on your lap, telling you about her day, but you miss all of it because you're trying to figure out the best way to respond to that email lingering in your inbox. Our attention is the most valuable gift we have to give.

Where are you giving yours?

And finally, when we're spiritually present, we can see the bigger picture, the truer one. Every minute is pregnant with the possibility of a happy moment. But many of us are sleepwalking through life, blind to all of it, too focused on the material world. Creation is conspiring to show us its best stuff, but to see it, you have to expand your horizon to the spiritual plane, beyond your email inbox, your phone, and your to-do list for the day. Wonder is everywhere.

Are your eyes open to it?

When we look back on a given year, it's easy to identify the massive oak trees and tall pines that stand as signposts: the weddings and the funerals, the epic vacations, and the major accomplishments.

But we often overlook the small blessings—the birds within the trees, if you will.

Thinking about and even recording our happy moments is a simple practice that makes it easier to spot those birds. When we invest a few seconds to jot down one happy moment a day, reading them at the end of the month or year is magical. It's like experiencing a sublime symphony, with each note harmoniously contributing its voice to a melody that slowly builds to a soaring crescendo of gratitude.

It becomes a **hallelujah chorus,** exulting the glorious gift of being alive.

And this, my friend, is the antidote to envy and fear and the ever-present feeling that we're not enough:

gratitude.

Too often, our eyes drift away from the wonder right in front of us, the must be nices in our midst. I wrote this book to encourage you to quit wishing for someone else's, find your own, and make the most of them. Hopefully this book helped you uncover at least 114 of them and inspired you to assemble them in ways only you can for the benefit of us all.

More than anything else, I hope it awakened you to the magic within you and the opportunities before you. No one knows what the future holds, but I can guarantee you this: the year ahead is bursting with possibilities for happy moments.

sun
sun
sun

here it comes

Like the one I had recently, when I surprised the kids with Dairy Queen Blizzards (Frosted Animal Cookie for me) before rolling through the automatic car wash. They delighted at the sight of the purple and blue "unicorn" soap and squealed in equal parts terror and delight when I suggested we roll down their windows. Alas, I did not. Maybe next time.

These happy moments are treasures, every last one of them.

I wish you the unhurried mind and clear eyes to see and appreciate them all.

Because every single one is a must be nice.

It's true: there are people with more money, more awards, and more notoriety than you, who take more vacations at more luxurious resorts. There are folks with less debt, smaller noses, and fewer obstacles than you. You may not have perfect health, the best hair, or the biggest house on the block, but there is something just as true:

You are rich beyond measure.

If you declutter your mind, clear your eyes, and pay attention, it will take you the whole day to count all the blessings of your charmed life.

Must be nice.

ESCAPE
ADULTHOOD

Drop Jason a line at
jason@escapeadulthood.com

For a treasure trove of Adultitis-fighting tips & tools,
or to learn more about bringing in Jason to speak
to your organization, skedaddle on over to
escapeadulthood.com

jason kotecki is a professional reminder-er and permission granter who moonlights as an artist, author and professional speaker. Jason and his wife Kim have made it their mission in life to help people and organizations break free from Adultitis to build better lives, businesses, and teams.

Jason has written eight books, and his colorful art has been collected and licensed all over the world. As a speaker, Jason works with organizations to beat burnout and become more innovative by breaking rules that don't exist. His content-rich programs are balanced with a refreshing mix of humor and emotion, serving as the perfect antidote for people who find themselves in a personal or professional rut.

Ultimately, Jason creates art, observations, and experiences that give people hope and the freedom to live joyfully. His greatest desire is to use his talents to share God's love and impact lives by inspiring, entertaining and encouraging people to rekindle their childlike spirit and create the lives they were made for.

An avid eater of sugar-laden cereal, Jason enjoys Star Wars, soft t-shirts, and brand new tubes of paint. He and Kim homeschool their three weird kids and live in Sheboygan, Wisconsin where they eat way too many cheese curds.

Jason's art has been collected by fans all over the world.
Browse the Lemonade Stand for a wide selection of prints,
greeting cards, t-shirts, originals and other
goodies featuring your favorite work
from Jason!

Visit EscapeAdulthood.com/shop

A sought-after keynote speaker, Jason has been hired by some of the world's largest organizations looking to increase morale, engagement, and innovative thinking. Recognized as a Certified Speaking Professional® by the National Speakers Association (a designation held by only 10% of speakers in the world), Jason's message reaches tens of thousands of people each year. His inspiring, engaging, and heart-warming programs are visual masterpieces jam-packed with relevant, practical information coated in fun that help people become more passionate, productive, and profitable.

Learn more at EscapeAdulthood.com/speaking

bushels of thanks

My books aren't like normal books, what with their whimsical style and abundance of color and pictures. Alas, I find myself unable to conform to the "serious" format of most books, which are pictureless, monochromatic, text-heavy, and quite often filled with fluff. Considering the fact that most adults don't read a single book after leaving school, perhaps this is a good thing.

Although my books may be difficult for some to take seriously, the challenge of impacting lives is one I take very seriously. My goal is to make a book so engaging that if someone picks it up, they want to keep reading it. In an attention-span starved world of Twitter and Tik Tok, the airy design and sense of humor makes the book more accessible to more people. And the images help people remember the life-changing concepts long after they put it down.

All this to say that if you bought this book for yourself, a friend, or a work colleague who is always complaining about how bad they have it, thank you. Not everyone gets what I'm trying to do here, but you do.

And that's one heck of a must be nice.

Of course there are many more must be nices that made this book possible, in the form of amazing and generous human beings, including the merry band of Adultitis Fighters and members of the Wonder & Whimsy Society, who have rallied around this mission and encourged me with their support.

And there's my editor Christina, who made this book better with her sharp eye and attention to detail.

And my Dream Team, including Sue and Jenna who have been there since the very beginning, and Rachel, whose enthusiasm has fueled new growth.

And Gary and Joyce, the best in-laws in history and whose faith inspires me.

And Mom and Dad, amazing parents who showed their three boys the secret to a rich life through their example of love, commitment, and sacrifice.

And Lucy, Ben, and Ginny, my awesome kids who give me new reasons to be grateful every day. I'm proud to be your dad.

And Kim, my wife, best friend, partner in crime, and biggest fan. I'm not sure what I did to deserve you, but you are my biggest must be nice.

And last but not least, to my heavenly Father, who has blessed me with more must be nices than I'll ever be able to count. **Soli Deo Gloria**

art & photo credits

All artwork in this book was created by Jason Kotecki.
Additional art and photo credits:

Phillip Larking, Unsplash (p IV)

Louis Hansel, Unsplash (p VI)

Jesus Eca, Unsplash (p 1)

Thomas M Evans, Unsplash (p 8)

Bobby McLeod, Unsplash (p 11)

Matt Briney, Unsplash (p 19)

Tyler Dunn (p 21)

Ethan, Unsplash (p 22)

Kim Kotecki (pp 27, 210, 212, 214)

Ivan Sanford, Unsplash (p 48)

Daniel Sinoca, Unsplash (p 64)

Ginny Kotecki (p 79)

Mae Mu, Unsplash (p 84)

Henry Be, Unsplash (p 86)

Dainis Graveris, Unsplash (p 88)

Esperanza Doronila, Unsplash (p 114)

Dim Gunger, Unsplash (p 116)

Pamela Lima, Unsplash (p 148)

Greg Rosenke, Unsplash (p 152)

Feliphe Schiarolli, Unsplash (p 154)

Supply Co, Unsplash (p 168)

Timothy Dykes, Unsplash (p 176)

Dave Adamson, Unsplash (p 184)

Strvnge Films, Unsplash (p 193)

Jason Richard, Unsplash (p 204)

Nikita Shirokov, Unsplash (p 206)

Nathan Dumlao, Unsplash (p 208)